EVENING
DELIGHTS

LALLAN PRASAD

PARTRIDGE
A Penguin Random House Company

To order additional copies of this book, contact
Partridge India
000 800 10062 62
www.partridgepublishing.com/india
orders.india@partridgepublishing.com

Dedicated to
Shri Shiv Shankar Vajpayee
My English Teacher

Acknowledgement

The Author gratefully acknowledges the support of Dr. Rajiva Verma, Dr. Pradeep Mathur, Dr. Dinesh Mishra, Mrs. Prem Lata, Dr. Anand Kesari, Sadanand Kesri and Dr. Rajesh Kesari

Foreword

This collection of poems came as a pleasant surprise to me: surprise, because though I had Known the author for several years as a colleague at Delhi University's South Campus, I had no inkling during all those years that he was not only interested in poetry but was himself a poet; pleasant, because the poems, apart from being a pleasure to read, demonstrated vividly the fact that the love of poetry is not confined to those who study or teach literature but cuts across all disciplines and professions. In his professional life Professor Lallan Prasad has been a distinguished teacher of business and economics, but in these poems he comes across not as a specialist but, to use the words used by Wordsworth to describe a poet, as 'a man speaking to men'.

The poems can be broadly divided, echoing Wordsworth again, into those dealing with the love of nature and those dealing with the love of man. The nature poems capture the beauty of the everyday world of nature with vividness and sensitivity but at the same time sound a warning note about environmental degradation and disaster, as in the poem 'River in the City'. As for the poems in the second category, they cover a wide range of relationships and emotions: familial, social and romantic. Some of the romantic poems, for example, 'The Balcony' capture moments of intimacy and intensity in our ordinary daily lives with great sensitivity, others such as 'I and You' and 'Rainbow in You', express romantic love through images drawn from nature. However the best poem of this kind, 'Ek sa Laga' appears not in the present volume but in the author's earlier collection of poems in Hindi, 'Bheer ki Anken'

T.S.Elliot argued many years ago that poetry in the modern age had to be obscure and difficult. An unfortunate consequence of this view was that it sometimes led to a kind of poetry which presented an intellectual challenge to the reader that was akin to that of a tough puzzle and the pleasure that it gave was the pleasure of satisfaction of having worked out the puzzle. Professor Lallan Prasad's poems are not of that kind. In spite of many lapses of idioms and usages they are eminently readable and the pleasure that they give is the pleasure of finding in them a reflection of our own common thoughts and feelings. Another way of describing the pleasure that these poems give is to compare it to the pleasure of conversation among friends and like-minded people, where there is a sharing of experiences without any attempt to dazzle or shock. In these days of loud assertion, therefore, many readers will welcome such a collection of poems.

Rajiva Verma
Former Head, Department of English
University of Delhi

Contents

1.	Acknowledgement	vi
2.	Foreword	vii
3.	Rooted Deep in the Soil	1
4.	Song of Nature	2
5.	An Evening Delight	3
6.	A Kiss	4
7.	Miles Long	5
8.	Not to Yield	6
9.	Trust	7
10.	I and You	8
11.	The Flower Queen	9
12.	Rejoice	10
13.	Night Bird	11
14.	Flower Show	12
15.	A Tribute	13
16.	Night Queen	14
17.	Tree Fairy	15
18.	Drawing Sheet	16
19.	Assembly of Poets	17
20.	The Planet	18
21.	A Thousand Flowers	20
22.	Burning Fire	21
23.	Blooming	22
24.	Whisper	23
25.	Who Cares?	24
26.	Little Squirrel	25
27.	Journey	26

28. Good Day 27

29. Season's Greetings 28

30. Treasure Within 29

31. Touch of Freshness 30

32. ADDICTION (Acrostic) 31

33. Together 32

34. Small Canvas 33

35. Season's Perfume 34

36. Time's March 35

37. City No More 36

38. SPRING IS COMING (Acrostic) 37

39. A Proud Mother 38

40. Rainbow 39

41. Caught 40

42. Envy 41

43. Red Roses 42

44. Season's Chill 43

45. St. Valentine's Day 44

46. Ever Flowing 45

47. The Glass House 47

48. The Beginning 48

49. Never to Part 49

50. Autumn's Leaf 50

51. Not to Be Shy 51

52. River in the City 52

53. Never to Return 53

54. Walk the Talk 54

55. Innocence 55

56. The Monsoon 56

57. Unimaginable 57

58. The Soul 58

59. The Honey 59
60. The Magnet 60
61. Rainbow in You 61
62. Away from the Crowd 62
63. Destiny 63
64. The Height 64
65. The Green God 65
66. With Love 67
67. In the Mirror 68
68. Shy 70
69. If I Were Rich 71
70. Banaras 72
71. Buddha 73
72. Jesus 74
73. Gandhi 75
74. Those in Power 76
75. Butterfly 77
76. Glory 78
77. Power Within 79
78. Pinkish Horizon 80
79. Standing Ovation 81
80. The Balcony 82
81. Images 83
82. Deep Agony 84
83. Co - exist 85
84. For Women 86
85. Eyes Invite 87
86. Ma 88
87. Inner Voice 89
88. Morning Paper 90
89. Sharing 91

90.	Timber	92
91.	Shining Glaciers	93
92.	Full Moon	94
93.	Where Parrots Talk	95
94.	Warm Touch	96
95.	First Glimpse	97
96.	Burning Myself	98
97.	Limit	99
98.	Tearing the Wind	100
99.	Reflections	101
100.	Evening Shadow	102
101.	Waves of Time	103
102.	An Island's Agony	104
103.	Come Night Come	106
104.	Angel and Devil	107
105.	Dark Clouds	108
106.	White Roses	109
107.	Blue Canopy	110
108.	Season of Love	111
109.	Little to choose	112
110.	Other Sides	113
111.	Inside	114
112.	Polluting Me	115
113.	The Light	117
114.	Cheers	118
115.	Revolution, Revolution . . .	119
116.	Precious	121
117.	Love Peace and Harmony	122

Rooted Deep in the Soil

Rooted deep in the soil
Firm on the ground
I am duty - bound to nourish
Hundreds of branches
Thousands of leaves
Birds and bees

I never feel shy
Under the blue sky
To face hot sun, cold waves
Storms and snowfalls
Mild showers and
Heavy rainfalls

I am born to give
Fruits and flowers
Shade and shelter to all
To pay my debt to mother earth
Whose love and care
I have enjoyed since birth.

Song of Nature

White bears playing on the snow
Falcons flying in a row

Clouds pouring mild showers
Winds teasing smiling flowers

Roses blooming amidst thorns
Birds caring for the newly born

Stars twinkling in the night
Golden moon shining bright

Sun retiring in the evening
Rising afresh in the morning

Birds on the branches singing
The song nature is composing.

An Evening Delight

In search of peace
Love and harmony
Two hearts meet
The sky and the ocean
Greet each other
Distance gone

Smiling horizon
A feast of colors
Pink, yellow, blue
Black and white
Clouds in the space
Limitless, infinite

Sun ready to retire
Waves waiting for
The last kiss of
The red golden rays
Reflecting bright
An evening delight.

A Kiss

When a butterfly gives a kiss
To a blooming red rose
Is it not the same
That happens to me
When your wet lips
Touch my soft cheeks?

Miles Long

When two hearts meet
And greet each other
Geometry fails
Love knows no bounds
Eyes play with color
Ears with musical sound

When one heart desires
But the other fires
Falling star leaves behind
Miles long trail
Vanishing at the end
No hope to mend.

Not to Yield

The mountain peak
Facing the hot summer
Lightning and thunderstorms
Snowfalls and avalanches
Asking its soldiers
— The long trees —
Not to yield, stand firmly
Take sportingly
The challenges of
The seasons
Asking no reasons
Bloom in the summer
Lush green leaves
Snow cover in the winter
Wait for the spring
To flower its valleys.

Trust

The sun trusts
The moon will come soon
As the darkness wraps
His bed in the night
With silver stars
All over in sight

The mountains trust
Clouds will come
And rain
Water all around
Jumping from the rocks
Making musical sound.

I and You

I am a flower
You are my color
My fragrance, my beauty

I am a river
You are my water
My flow, my purity

I am a bird
You are my wings
My songs, my flight

I am the sky
You are my sun
My moon, my light.

The Flower Queen

Color from the moon
Brightness from the sun
Softness from the soil
Freshness from the wind
You bring together
Champa, the flower queen

Brides love you
Young ladies smile
When you are in their
Wet hair for a while
Mothers dream daughters
To be named after you

When you are on a branch
Green leaves surround you
Butterflies kiss you
Winds carry your message
With sweet perfume
From garden to bedroom.

Rejoice

Fishes envy your eyes
Butterflies your ears
Lilies your color
Clouds your hair

Flowers envy your face
Apples your cheeks
Deer your skin
Cherries your lips

Birds envy your voice
Friends your choice
In all that all envy in you
I love and rejoice.

Night Bird

A bright eyed smiling night bird
Finds the guys — prey to night
When darkness will not let
The light come anywhere near it
Making flight unseen unnoticed
Will land on the tree hiding the nest
Where baby birds are taking rest
Walk on the branch slowly and slowly
Pounce on them violently
Caring least for their mom's protest
And have a wonderful feast.

Flower Show

In a flower show of roses
The bright ones were boasting
And the dull were depressed
The red were arrogant
The pink were mild and
The yellow were graceful

The mixed color roses
Were humble
The bigger flowers were wild
Keeping their branches
Under pressure all the time
Little ones looked like a child

The white roses were
Calm and quiet
A pure delight.

A Tribute

The invisible painter has all the colors
And canvas of a size we can't measure

Which color to use, when and where
He knows and decides with great care

He pours gold on the sea shores
Every morning and evening

He prints the rainbow in seven colors
From one end of the horizon to the other

He paints the landscape green
Flowers and fruits in multicolor

Mountain peaks are painted white
To reflect the bright sun light.

Night Queen

White flowers bloom
When the Night Queen
Takes the day away
Into her bedroom.

Tree Fairy

When a fairy descends
From the blue sky
The first resting place for her
Is the tall green tree
With soft shining leaves
On big and small branches
Colorful flowers blooming
Attracting honeybees
Sweet fragrance in the air
When she lands there
In a rainbow color robe
Silky shining long hair
Sitting on the tree
She locates a school
Looks with curiosity
At the ringing bell
The playground
Full of lovely children
For whom she came
All the way from heaven.

Drawing Sheet

Given a home task by their teacher to draw
the picture of a beautiful butterfly
Most children did so, but some
Caught living ones from the park nearby

Pasted them on their drawing sheets,
The poor creatures who don't ever cry
Met early death helplessly in silence
None was there to bid them goodbye.

Assembly of Poet

I had a dream
I built a castle in the air
With windows wide open
For winds to carry fragrance
From the big garden around
With green trees and roses
Of all colors blooming
Birds singing the song of nature
Bees humming, butterflies
Kissing flowers wildly.

At the house warming —
My friends were there
In traditional dresses
Exchanging greetings
Reciting their choicest poems
Enjoying Italian opera
Folk songs and music
Indian classical dances
Food and drink of their taste
No one was in haste.

Night passed, the dream was through
I wish it had been true.

The Planet

The vast and lovely planet we live in
Is full of contrasts
Civilizations built brick by brick,
Some are flourishing, some lost

Big mountains, deep valleys,
Hard rocks, soft sands,
Snowy peaks, long deserts,
Green fields, dry lands

Roaring lions, lovely deer,
Big elephants, little ants,
Flowing rivers, sleeping pools,
Zooming trees, small plants

Deep seas, shallow waters,
Big sharks, gold fishes,
Flying birds, creeping insects,
Dark nights, bright days

Roses with thorns
Seasons warm, seasons cold
Pouring rains, dry spells,
Mild showers, thunderbolts

Happiness and sorrow
Richness and poverty
Overfeeding and hunger
Slavery and liberty

Differences in languages
Customs and traditions
Religions and rituals
Beliefs and faiths

Yet a unity in diversity
Mother earth's children
Sharing nature's fruits and
Living, enjoying life together.

A Thousand Flowers

A hundred flowers will bloom
The day you say 'yes'
The day you put
Your hand in mine
The day you walk with me
On the sea shore
Waves kissing our feet
Celebrating our first meeting

A hundred flowers will bloom
The day you run with me
After the butterflies
Flying to kiss roses, and
Listen to the little birds
Singing on branches of trees
Morning breeze moving
With humming bees.

A thousand flowers will bloom
The day you are with me
Depriving even the moon
Of having a glimpse of us
With curtains on, in the room
Jasmine spreading fragrance
Two souls getting warm
The mirror reflecting your charm.

Burning Fire

I am not a mirror to reflect you
As you think you are
I have my own ideas and inspirations
Interests, dreams and desires
Within me is a burning fire
Which I can't extinguish
To be at peace with you at any cost
Even though at times I may feel lost.

Blooming

Love blooming in the heart,
Hate brewing in a corner of the mind
Dreams awakening during the night,
Desires aspiring to explore

Poetry, the golden means of
Expressing emotions, aspirations
Sentiments and feelings
But not perversions.

Whisper

A little black bird
Flying by my side
Whispers in my ear:
"Come with me
The sky is vast
Open your wings
Touch the horizon."

Who Cares?

Who cares about the writing on the wall
When every wall is destined to fall?

Flowers blooming with pride
Petals to leave in a few hours

Trees aiming to reach the sky
Bound by the limits of height

Rivers coming from snow peaks
Going to merge with the sea

Mountains with sleeping volcanoes
Hot lava to cover any day

Soldiers with marching orders
Death awaiting in the field

Rulers committing atrocities
People's revolts to bring their fall

Parents fighting and divorcing
Children deprived of love and care

Carved on stone, written in books
History read and forgotten.

Little Squirrel

A little squirrel
Going up and down the tree
Jumping and running free
Picking nuts and berries
Tasting, eating creamy layers
With both hands
Leaving nuts on the ground
Ears alert, eyes moving
Looking around
Bushy tail up
Sudden storm!
An eagle from the sky
Catches by the neck
Flies to
A destination unknown
End of a playful life.

Journey

Thrown in a dustbin
Taken to the factory
Crushed and processed
Born as paper
Bought by an artist
Brushed with rainbow colors
Framed in gold
Placed in an art gallery
Seen, loved and admired.

Good Day

Bright morning
Fresh fragrant flowers
Wishing a good day.

Season's Greetings

Mild showers in spring
Sweet fragrance from the soil
Birds spreading their feathers
Dancing and bathing
Young plants zooming
Green leaves shining

Clouds covering the sun
A light breeze blowing
Fragile flowers shaking
Petals falling down
Little frogs jumping
Silky hares running

Couples on the sea shore
Embracing and kissing
Seagulls flying above
Waves coming nearer
Giving the lovers
The season's greetings.

Treasure Within

A treasure lies within
We fail to discover
Intoxicated we are
Not only by the wine
But the glasses too
Made by others.

Heart we want to confine
To circulating the blood
Not to interfere in
Recognizing the voice
Feelings, intentions and
Emotions of others

When we stretch legs
Beyond the bed
And refuse to listen to others
Blow hot and cold
We deprive ourselves
Of love — the real gold.

When we realize
What others say
And listen to our inner self
We need no more help
To judge ourselves and
Play our destined roles.

Touch of Freshness

When we bend to dig the soil and sow the seeds
We give a tribute to nature
Its plants and trees, butterflies and bees
We get our own knees oiled
Pray to mother earth to give birth
To tender branches and green leaves.

When we shower water on the plants
We pull our weight and for days we wait
For lovely buds to open their petals
Full of colors and perfume
Inviting flies to come and kiss
A chance they would never like to miss.

When we walk in the early morning
We feel the first touch of freshness
Blessings and selflessness
Little birds singing, dancing and
Jumping from one branch to other
Tasting choicest fruits and flowers.

When we sit on a bench to relax
We find the dew drops have disappeared
The murmuring leaves whisper in our ears —
The garden is green, air is fresh
Get ready, open your heart
A promising new day is going to start.

ADDICTION (Acrostic)

A state of drunkenness
Desire soaring high
Decline in memory, blurred vision
Insanity taking over
Coming pleasure alluring
Tall promises made
Irrational behavior demanding
Once more, only once more
Not caring for the consequences.

Together

A home is blessed
Where all in the family live together
Talk to each other
Share a common dining table
And distress and life's pleasure

The grandma and pa are blessed
Who have company of little angels
Tell them the fairy tales
Become their horses
Put them on their backs

The couples are blessed
Who sing and dance together
Keep their ego cool
Care for each other's emotions
Have tolerance and patience.

The children are blessed
Whose parents love them
Give them all they desire
Keep them on their eyebrows
Let them play and grow.

The sun, the moon and
The stars share one sky
"Family ties can't survive" why?

Small Canvas

The canvas is small
The horizon is large
I can't catch it all

The sky is full of colors
The sun is going to set
I have limited paints

Winds are blowing
Birds are flying back
My brush is slowing.

Season's Perfume

Cuckoos know it well
Now is the time to sing
Butterflies are dancing
Bees are forming the ring.

Flowers are blooming
All over mango trees
Wild winds are getting
Season's perfume free.

Leaves are thickening
The sun is getting hotter
The rivers are flowing gently
With clean fresh water.

Time's March

Soldier's footprints,
Drumbeats and gun fires
All become history
Remaining in memory
Destructions caused
Relations strained
Pains suffered

Only time's march continues
Unabated, nonstop
Washing tears, healing the wounds
Regenerating, rebuilding
Lighting the dark streets again
Staging life's drama
Bringing smiles back from exile

Creating simultaneously
New battalions to march
Beat the drums again
Fire and destroy
Take away
The moments of glory
Happiness and joy.

City No More

Tears rolling on the wet cheeks
A mother of two
Standing before the shattered walls
No windows, no roof
Empty street, no noise
Where once was her home

Parents and children
Whom she had promised
To come back soon
Were swallowed by
The cruel Tsunami
Which came when she was away

Her searching eyes
Where are they? Where are they?
Folded hands looking towards the sky
She was crying why? why?
The shivering body fell unconscious
Carried by an ambulance

The city was no more
But the waves were still roaring
On the sea shore.

SPRING IS COMING (Acrostic)

Spring is coming
Pools are flooding with the water birds
Rising sun is calling falcons to fly high
In the clean blue sky
Nests are getting empty
Gone are the cold winds and the waves
Inside forests trees are zooming and
Shadowing the earth

Colorful flowers are blooming
On the branches everywhere
Moving with the fragrant air
Inviting the butterflies
Near and near
Greeting them in the mating season.

A Proud Mother

I am a proud mother
Of seven billion human beings
The most intelligent species
Excelling in art and architecture
Music and dance, science and technology
I give them all they need
For a life style of their choice

I am a proud mother of the seasons
Summer, winter, autumn and spring
Farms, forests and trees
Mountains with glaciers
Having the first kiss of sunshine
Flowers and flies with color combines

Winds spreading fragrance
Birds singing and dancing
Lions roaring, the deer running
Peacocks dancing, falcons flying
Cats mewing, bears playing
All enjoying life under my care.

Rainbow

Colors in
The life's rainbow
One end to the other —
Happiness, sorrow
Laughter, fear
Love, hate and anger.

Caught

A spider weaves a net
The fly caught in
Flutters till end.

Envy

White roses
kissed by
the shy silver butterflies
envy
colorful spring flowers
surrounded by
more colorful
silky sleek shining
butterflies.

Red Roses

Red roses
Nicely kept in a flower pot
In the corner of a room
Were thinking —
If we were not plucked
Out of our branches
We would have been
Under the open sky
Surrounded by
Beautiful butterflies
Breathing fresh air
In mother plant's loving care.

Season's Chill

From the valley
To the top of the hill
The season's chill
Has grounded —
Men and women
Animals and birds
No voice is heard
No sound echoes
In the kingdom of silence.

Lights have lost brightness
In the foggy night's darkness
Things are at a standstill
Except love
Which has free play
In theatres and
In the bedrooms
With the honeymooning
Brides and bridegrooms
Who are in no hurry
To welcome
The arrival of morning
Movements on the street
And the bright sun in the sky.

St. Valentine's Day

Let lilies and lotuses
see our hearts blooming
Let cuckoos and nightingales
Listen to us singing.

Let gold and silver fishes
See us swimming in the river
Which the blue sky has been using
As an unframed mirror.

Let fresh winds touch us
Take our perfume to spread
Let kisses make our lips
All the more red.

Let St. Valentine's day bring
The season's blessings
Surprises and greetings
For the lovers in waiting.

Ever Flowing

Every day is a birthday
I am born and reborn
I am an ever flowing river
With origin in melting glaciers
Ending into the limitless sea.

When I am on the hills
I enjoy playing with rocks
I fall and get shocks.
When on the plains
I have a smooth walk.

Within the banks
Of my own creation,
I nourish plants and trees
Birds, animals, humans
And lovely fishes.

When in anger I may
Endanger all habitats
Flooding cities, towns, villages
Breaking rules of the game
I know I get a bad name.

When crazy people
Put me behind their
Dams of concrete
Difficult for me to delete
I still fight with all my might.

I know it well
Growth and decline,
Success and failure,
Flow with me unabated
For which I am created.

The Glass House

A thought which is
My brain child
Close to my heart
I will nourish it even
In the glass house
To save it from falling apart
Blocking all attempts
To put it out in the cold
The mother in me
With her love and care
Will see it blooming
Amidst all odds,
Smiling and playing.

The Beginning

Give your hands in mine
Come closer and closer to me
Let my eyes see in your eyes
Kiss me and let me kiss not once
But as many times as we missed
Since we met first
It is only the beginning of the thirst

Tell me how many nights
You could not sleep because of me
What made you weep
I am here with you
To say sorry and wipe out your tears
To heal your wounds and listen to you,
To be yours and one with you forever.

Never To Part

When in despair think of a river
The journey it takes to flow forever

Coming from glaciers kissing the rocks
Singing dancing never afraid of blocks

Broadening its banks in a mood to play
From difficult terrains making its way

Jumping from hills roaring waterfalls
Turning hard stones into lovely balls

Passing through jungles and the plains
Taking together the water from the rains

Giving life to all whether big or small
Fishes birds plants humans and animals

Travelling miles and miles no fatigue
Meeting and marrying the mighty sea

Embracing its beloved heart to heart
Flowing continuously never to part.

Autumn Leaf

Love me not
If you don't feel
The warmth of my touch,
If you don't believe
The promises I make
I don't want our love
To be an autumn leaf
Which may eventually fall
After floating in the air.

Not to Be Shy

In the full moon night,
On the bank of the river
When we met first
On promise to be together.

The night queen's fragrance
The soft cool breeze
The murmuring of trees
The humming of bees
The twinkling stars
In the dark blue sky
Were all calling us
Not to be shy, not to be shy.

Then your strong arms
Touched me gently
And your red lips
Were kissing me freely
Eyes into eyes
Arms into arms
We came closer and closer
As never before.

Breathing restlessly
Feeling the warmth
We became one
To be together forever.

River in the City

A city of millions at the mercy of a river
Which looked like a canal a few days earlier

It flooded suddenly after years of rest
The city had to pay its debts with interest

The river has taken over the city from its mayor
Water on streets and in houses everywhere

Islands have come up here and there
A scene the city dwellers never witnessed

The river has called planners at the door
Nature is giving warning to us once more

Leave my rivers to flow, my forests to grow
Or else the concrete jungles will be no more.

Never to Return

A rain drop never
Goes back to the cloud,
A leaf never returns to the branch
Once blown out.

A rose petal fallen on the ground
Is lost forever
A river meeting the sea
loses its flowing water.

A love lost which breaks hearts
Keeps the two souls apart.

Walk the Talk

Men and women
Who make history
Are no different from us
In their flesh and blood
And the physical chemistry.

They have the
Courage of conviction
They walk the talk
They live on the ground
Not in fiction.

No sacrifice is big
For these devoted souls
Be it the physical comfort
Or life itself
To achieve their goals.

They leave the world
Better than what they inherit
They are remembered
By generations
Purely on their merit.

Innocence

Dear rose
You are so innocent and loving
The bee comes to you humming
And showering praise
You open with all the grace
He gives you momentary pleasure
And leaves to mate with another flower.

The charming shy butterfly
On whom you always rely
Comes and gives you a deep kiss
But leaves you soon to miss
The pleasure of being together
You seek you desire.

The wind passing by
Touches you gently,
Making you to shiver
Takes your fragrance for others,
Goes away, you are shaken
You are broken.

The monsoon

The journey of clouds
From ocean to the sky
Tons of water for
Forests and mountains high

Thunder and lightning
Heavy showers pouring
Sun hiding behind
Clouds darkening.

Water falling from the rocks
Rivers flooding
Grasses and plants
Sprouting and greening.

Animals mating in the open
Young birds peeping from
Holes of the trees
Eagles enjoying the flying.

Farmers sowing the seeds
Singing and dancing
Clouds over clouds in the sky
Thundering and raining.

Unimaginable

When a kite is in the sky
It is no more shy
It enjoys the flight
As a falcon at the height
Unimaginable unbelievable.

When the flyer commands
It goes to fight other kites
With all its might.
If it succeeds it roots them out
If it fails in the bout
It loses its string
As a thrown ring,
Not knowing where will it fall
On the top of a tree or
In a valley losing all.

It may get a new lease of life
If it kisses the ground
Where a new flyer picks it up
And prepares for a second round,
It will get a chance
To be again in the sky
Without being shy,
Reaching the height
Unimaginable unbelievable.

The Soul

The body is made of five elements:
Fire, water, air, ether and earth
From a Mother's womb it takes birth.

The soul is the power, the force
Eternal imperishable unseen
Always pure and clean.

It cannot be cut by weapons
Burnt by fire, blown by winds
It never retires, lives forever.

The soul enters the body at birth
When it leaves, the body is dead
Blood is no more red.

When the body dies all organs fail
The elements finally retire
No matter whether we bury it or
Give it to fire.

The Honey

Bees know where the honey lies
They don't kiss all the flowers
They know which ones will bloom
In the garden at which hours.

They know when the buds will
Open their petals, invite for mating
Spreading fragrance all around
Without waiting for dating.

The Magnet

When you are in my arms
And my lips are on your cheeks
You become a magnet
No flower can steal your beauty
No perfume can match your fragrance
No music can be sweeter than your voice
Leaving for me no choice
But to take you to bed
Make your lips all the more red.
You become the wave of an ocean
With all your might
You become one with me
As full moon and moon light.

Rainbow in You

I saw a rainbow in you at last
Making me to forget all
That happened
Between us in the past.

The rainbow of colors
Of roses, lilies, tulips
Your eyes and wet lips
After a deep kiss

The rainbow from
One horizon to another
Overshadowing me
After heavy showers

The rainbow in you
Dispelling all my doubts
After thunders and lightning
From the black clouds

Away From the Crowd

At times
Loneliness is bliss
As sweet as a kiss
Away from the crowd
On the bank of a river
Flowing gently
Waves of thought
Coming suddenly
Urging to create
Something
As beautiful as
A blooming red rose
As charming as
A fairy queen
As sweet as
The morning breeze
Entering the room unseen.

Destiny

We call Destiny
That which may not be in our hands
Which comes from the blue
Of which we have no clue

The scriptures tell us
What we sow we reap
Our Karmas of the past
Make us laugh and weep

We have moments of joy
Opportunities showered
We also have times critical
When things are difficult

Scientists argue — no destiny
Believe not what can't be proved
By logic and experimentation
Decide your own destination.

The Height

When an eagle goes up
It leaves behind
A vast landscape
It enters the sky
With infinite space
Over its little head
Left and right,
Winds do challenge
Its wings, its might,
But it wins with feathers
So flexible and light
Minutes of flying
It reaches the height
Comes back home easily
Without losing the sight.

The Green God

We offer prayer
In churches, temples and mosques
We carve His statues
In marble rocks
We fight in His name
Sending waves of shock.

We fail to see Him
In His marvelous creations
In the beauty of nature
His true manifestations
In living beings
With loving relations.

We don't notice
The vastness of the horizon
The dark clouds
On the peaks of mountains
The fields in the plain
Full of grain,

We don't feel His presence
In green plants and pastures
In dense forests fruits and
Colorful flowers
Waterfalls jumping from hills
And the flowing rivers.

We are turning green creations
Into jungles of concrete
Making the ozone layer
Continuously depleted
Inviting calamities to
Come and meet us.

With Love

My dear
When I took the pen
To write to you
I didn't know
Where to begin?

The day I met you first
Your eyes were shy
Your cheeks were red
You did not speak
Nor could I.

When you came closer
Months of exposure
Your words became
A source of pleasure
Your eyes began
To rest in my eyes
Like an invaluable treasure.

When you allowed
The first touch
With fragrance of
A hundred flowers
I forgot where had gone
The minutes and the hours.
With love
Yours forever.

In the Mirror

The clouds make
A solemn promise
To the moon
Not to block her
When she is
Looking at her face
In the mirror
Down the river.

But as soon as
She comes out
They cover her
The game of
Hide and seek
Depresses her
By the time
The clouds wither
Night is gone.

She has to
Wait and wait
For hours,
Till the day passes
The hot sun crosses
The horizon
Leaving place
For the darkness
To come and cover
The whole sky
Let the moon try
Have a glimpse
Again in the mirror
Down the river.

Shy

The clouds on
The east horizon
Are a little shy
When they see
Your lips red
Which I did
Just before I came
Out of the bed.

If I were Rich

If I were rich
I would have built a mansion
In a dense forest
I would enjoy watching
What nature has given
Without asking
Colorful flowers
Birds dancing singing
Feeding their little ones
In the nest
Lions taking rest

Rivers making waterfalls
Going down the hills
Trees hiding the earth
Animals giving birth
In the open
Monkeys picking fruits
Crocodiles swimming
Baby elephants walking
With mother, father

The evening sun
Taking away
Its golden rays
From tree tops
Mountain peaks
Saying good bye.

Banaras

An ancient city
A mosaic of cultures
Dances and music
Languages and literature
Art and architecture

A city of temples
An abode of Lord Shiva
A place to pray and
Bathe in the holy Ganga

A home of crafts
Customs and rituals
A seat of learning
Saints and philosophers.

Buddha

In every century
The likes of Angulimal
Tried to kill you
But alive you are,
Forgiving them all
Smiling you are

In the present century
With hammers and rods,
The Taliban broke your statue
In broad daylight
With the whole world
Watching the awful sight
But O' loving God
You are not shaken.

You remain unaffected
By violence of any kind
With no feeling of revenge
With heart so kind
You continue to shower
Your blessings
On all mankind
Sitting on the lotus flower.

Jesus

When we love Jesus
We should love humanity
Love even our enemies
Forgive them for their sins
Help those in need
Bring smile on the faces in fear
Wipe out their tears

When we love Jesus
We should love peace
Even at the cost of
Our own blood
As did Jesus
Forgiving those
Who nailed him to bleed.

Gandhi

An apostle of truth
Loved and admired by all
A pure heart
With malice towards none
Shook a mighty empire
No swords, no guns
Protests peaceful
Millions followed
To liberate India
Liberate world from
The colonial rule
Oppression and exploitation.

Those in Power

All revolutions begin with
Challenging those in power
In the tug of war
One side has the might
The other is exploited
Discriminated against and deprived
Violence and the non - violence
Are the weapons to fight

Gandhi won freedom for India
Through peaceful protests
Against a mighty empire
He walked the talk
So did Martin Luther King
Nelson Mandela and many others
The war continues
Against the tyranny of the state
In many parts of the world even today.

Butterfly

With your small wings
You fly gently
From one plant to another
Kissing every flower
Enjoying every moment
The fragrance
The beauty the color
Flowers wait for you
When you are late
They send the date
By wind passing by
You feel shy
When sunshine is mild
You go wild
Blooming buds are shaken
When overtaken.

Glory

Glory lies in becoming a mountain
Covered with clouds and snow all the year round
Giving birth to the source of life the rivers
Irrigating and greening fields and forests

Glory lies in becoming a tree with
Roots in the ground and branches in the sky
Facing hot sun, cold waves and storms
Yet giving nourishing fruits and flowers

Glory lies in becoming a forest with
Difficult terrains, hills and waterways
Sustaining a variety of flora and fauna
Lions, tigers, elephants, bears and the deer

Glory lies in becoming a poet, a writer
Expressing feelings and emotions
Ideas and concepts frankly fearlessly
Changing the very course of history

Glory lies in becoming an architect
Turning stones into inspiration,
A scientist inventing truths unknown
A leader to walk the talk

Glory lies in becoming a beloved wife
A caring mother and a nourishing father
A loving and playful son or daughter
A reliable all weather friend.

Power Within

Eagles fly in sky
Mirror clean or cloudy
Seagulls are over the sea
Waves calm or rowdy.

The deer live in forests
Where hungry lions roar
Bears climb mountains
Dry or snowy shores.

Small fishes survive
With sharks around
Sleeping volcano
Green plants surround.

Writers pen at will
criticize or admire
soldiers march amidst
tanks and Gunfire.

Pinkish horizon

Bright morning sun
Pinkish horizon
Desire of branches
To reach the sky
Making them rise.
Fresh winds
Shaking hands with leaves
Colorful flowers zooming
On tender support
Without fear of falling.

Standing Ovation

The majestic river
Winds moving gently
Intoxicating fragrance
Waves parading
Sands shining
Holding firmly
Trees on the banks watching
Giving standing ovation
Falcons saluting from the sky
Life's flow unabated.

Storm comes
Winds get wings
Waves become tides
Sands slip
Some trees uprooted
Falcons fall
Death and destruction rule.

Storm withers
Winds and waves tired
Retire in peace
Sands holding again
Falcons open wings
Trees not uprooted smile
Life's flow begins afresh.

The Balcony

The sun rises first in my balcony
I don't know why?
The clouds on the east horizon are shy
When they see your lips red
Which I did before I came out of bed
The morning breeze brings fragrance
Before you open your eyes
Darkness leaves saying you goodbye
When I stand in the balcony
Leaving your shattered bed sheet
Your uncombed silky hair
The lotus flowers in the pool below
Begin to bloom, roses smile.

Images

Come as a flash
Any time anywhere
Taking me unaware
Filling up pages in my diary
Putting my signature
And disappear.

Deep Agony

The flourishing eyes
Of rich and powerful
Never realize
The deep agony of
The depressed, the deprived
And the discriminated.

Co - exist

An open
Large hearted sky
Millions of stars
Co - exist
Moving freely
Fearlessly
On their axes
Shining brightly.

For Women

Heaven for men
Hell for women
Is it God given?
Cleaning, washing
Cooking and caring
In women's lot
Power, authority
Handsome pay
Men have got
Women excelling
In profession are
Islands in the ocean
They are denied rights
For which
They have to fight.

Eyes Invite

Eyes love, eyes hate
Eyes open or close the gate to the heart.

Eyes speak, eyes silence
Eyes may be on the fence to get close or apart.

Eyes invite, eyes refuse
Eyes make an excuse to act or play smart.

Ma

Ma
You gave me life
The safest place on earth
When in the womb
You made sacrifices
Which only you could
Losing your physical charm
Keeping me fit and warm
Your concern for me
Never dwindled in life
In illness, in depression
You have always been
A source of inspiration.

Inner Voice

We are spiritual
When we listen to
The voice of our soul
Which lead us to
The desirable goals

We know
Trees don't eat their own fruit
Cows don't drink their own milk
Let us serve our sisters, brothers
Birds, animals and nature

Let us listen to
Our inner voice
Broaden our choice
Love and be loved
And rejoice.

Morning Paper

The black letters get red
When I turn the pages of
The morning news paper

A bomb blast in a crowded market
A terrorist organization taking credit
A murder in the city
Police hunting for the criminal
An accident taking precious lives
Survivors in pain in the hospital
A traveler robbed in daylight
No one coming to rescue
A body found hanging in a room
Suicide note pasted on the wall
A ministry report claiming
Fall in the crime rate

Violence, violence and violence
Overshadowing news
Which could be in colors?
Cream, pink, green or gold
My tea gets cold
So do I.

Sharing

Sitting in the office or at home
On a bench in a park or
On a remote hill top
Moving your fingers
On the little laptop
You write on my wall
I feel the warmth
Of your company
Reading on screen every line
More exciting than any wine
Distance no barrier
In meeting of minds and hearts
No visa, no restrictions
Face to face we are
Sharing what we desire
What we love and want to show
What we want to know.

Timber

I am timber
Value me as you wish
Burn me you get ash
Turn me into a pillar
You will have support
Make me a window
You invite fresh air
Use me as a boat
You float on the river
Build a home with me
You will be warm in winter
Cool in the summer
Carve an image on me
With chisel and hammer
Showcase your skill
Feeling and imagination
Paint me with colors of love
You will earn laurels.

Shining Glaciers

On the bank of
Mansarovar Lake in Tibet
Snow clad mountain peaks
All around
Biting cold during night
Dark blue sky
A full moon of the size
Not seen on the plains
No vegetables
No birds or animals in sight
Away from
The maddening crowd
A kingdom of peace
Crystal clear water
Shining glaciers reign.

Full Moon

A full moon
Floating gold in the river
Sun hidden behind
The dark blue sky
Waiting to rob.

Where Parrots Talk

Give me a house
Where I can live
With green plants around
Bird's musical sound
Fountain flowing
Fresh wind blowing

Give me a house
Where morning sun
Makes me awake
A cup of Darjeeling tea
In a silver tray
Beginning of a new day

Give me a house
Where parrots talk
Hares hide and run
Children have fun
Vegetables grow
Season's flower show.

Warm Touch

All leaves are destined to fall
Part with the mother tree
Most float in the air
Go down and stare
A few get a warm touch of
Caring and loving fingers.

First Glimpse

Early morning
Leaves on the top of trees
Welcome golden rays
Of the rising sun

Buds begin to open
Soft petals
Inviting butterflies
For the first kiss

Dew drops on the
Lush green glasses
Shine as little pearls
Before fading away

Birds come out of nests
Making lovely sound
Sweet winds spreading
Fragrance all around.

Burning Myself

Realm of thoughts
Blowing its own logic
Searching alternatives
Creating new ones
Eyes closed
In a dreamland
Swimming deep
In the past
Imagining future
Waves of Ideas
Coming, floating, going
Not known where?

Am I burning —
What I don't want?
What I don't care?
Or
Burning myself
Slowly and slowly.

Limit

Mountains
With great determination
Go up
But their high peaks
Get covered with snow
Trees rise to some height
And have to stop
Birds fly in the sky
But have to return
To their nests
The sky puts a limit for all.

Tearing the Wind

Flying at a high altitude
Looking for the prey
Miles away
Sharp shining eyes
Wings moving up and down
Tearing the wind
With speed and precision
Reaching the target
Leaving no time
For the poor creature

To hide or run
My dear eagle
For you it's a fun
You are bold
Not afraid of cold
On mountain peaks
You fly over vast oceans
Rivers and jungles
Feeling always at home
On the ground
At the tree tops
In the clouded sky
Wherever you are
You never feel shy.

Reflections

The light of life
Reflections sharp and bright
Longing to live long
Keeping the blood
Red and strong
Seeking the company of
A trusted, beloved, pure heart
Never playing smart
Melting base of age
Darkness at the bottom
Not to make afraid
Flames to burn till the end.

Evening Shadow

Large trees
On the bank of a river
Branches spread, green leaves,
Chatting birds, humming bees
Crimson flowers, sweet breeze
Looking on the shadow moving
Crystal clear water flowing
Silver fishes jumping, swimming
Evening sun gradually setting.

Waves of Time

A ray of hope ignites
To strive for what we want
We may dream of angels
Coming from sky to bless
But things may not happen
As we wish and desire
Plans and strategies
Prepared with great care
May not materialize
Causing disappointment

Life's boat sails
On the waves of time
Not always in the
Direction we desire
But by the winds
We can't control
Friends may desert
When needed most
Help may come from
Quarters unexpected
Lessons learnt are forgotten
Perfection is never reached.

An Island's Agony

Far from the maddening crowd
Surrounded by the sea all around
Green plants and long palm trees
Sweet flowers and humming bees
Young roses and roaming butterflies
Shallow water and shining eyes
Swimming gold and silver fishes
Coming true dreams and wishes
Couples enjoying without fear
Fresh perfume distributing air
Carefree children jumping playing
Birds chatting, singing and dancing
Occasional rains, pleasant showers
Happy inhabitants, blooming nature
I was a paradise on earth
Before greedy politicians took birth
Governments were formed
Corrupt and greedy men stormed
Killing my dear animals and birds
Committing atrocities never heard
Felling mercilessly green trees
Polluting pools, rivers and seas
Terrorists having a blood bath
Blocking on gun point the peace path

My inhabitants lost their freedom
Forced to live in a dreadful kingdom
Betrayal unforgettable, painful memory
Living in exile and a realm of slavery
Good days seem are gone for ever
Will I recover from the shock ever?

Come Night Come

Come night come
With shining silver stars
Smiling golden moon
Dancing on the floor of
The majestic Calm River

Come night come
Sun has already set
In the deep sea
Waves are rising
Running to the shore

Come night come
Seagulls are flying low
Dark velvet pallet
Will cover soon
Fields, forests, homes

Come night come
Let people recover
From the day's worry
Retire to bed
Let couples uncover.

Angel and Devil

The angel and the devil
Both live within us
Some of us follow
One of them
Some of us use both
As it suits us
All scriptures and saints
Inspired us to take
Right path, yet
The exploitation and torture
Of The weak by the powerful
Continues the world over.

Dark Clouds

White clouds
Floating in the sky
Never bring rains

Dark clouds
Rising from the sea
Threatening and lightning
Hide the sun
Stop its rays coming down
Conquer and
Cover the horizon
Flooding rivers
Fields and streets
Making their presence
Felt everywhere.

White Roses

You symbolize
Love, peace and tranquility
Why should I feel guilty?
When success eludes me
Even after doing my best
You show the way

You are always
On the bed of thorns
Since you are born
You face hot sun
Shivering cold
Sharp sting of bees
But remain playful
Invite butterflies
For a sweet kiss
Which they would
Never miss
Even when you decay
You leave white petals
Spread on the ground.

Blue Canopy

How soon will moon
Come in the sky?
Stars in silver robes
Are no more shy
Waiting to surround
With twinkling eyes
Rivers showing a mirror
All open no lies
Buds opening petals
Soft sweet breeze
Under the blue sky
Birds mating on trees
Lovers getting ready
For the great kiss.

Season of Love

Festival of colors organized by the spring
Birds from nests invited to sing

Butterflies dancing around the flowers
Light cool wind, occasional showers

Winter is gone, sun shining, warming
Snow has melted, seeds are sprouting

New born leaves look so charming
Fields, forests, pastures all greening

Season of love, dating and mating
Spring has arrived, no more waiting.

Little to choose

Who is fully secured?
A forest grown over hundreds of years
Wild fire can destroy it in hours
A big tree firmly rooted in the ground
A storm can uproot it any moment
A flourishing city with millions living happily
An earthquake can turn it into rubble
A life born and brought up with great care
Death can take it any time any where

We are as mortal as any object of nature
Any living specie in the universe
Our insecurity stems from within also
Emotions, feelings, likings, disliking
Which we don't express freely
Fear of discrimination, victimization
Exploitation hurt us deeply, yet
Political, social and legal conditions
Block our freedom to act
We may have little to choose.

Other Sides

Promises by leaders
With no intention to fulfill
Preaching by God men
With no faith in God
Smile on faces
With interior motive

A show of strength
By the physically weak
A kiss only to miss
With no desire to carry
Relationship into the future
Are other sides
Of the picture.

Inside

Inside every egg
A life is waiting in the dark
To see the day light
Breathe in fresh air
The life which symbolizes
The desire of two souls
To become one
In a state of bliss
The joys of the kiss
Warmth and pleasure
None can ever measure.

Polluting Me

I met a river and asked
How do you look upon the human race?
She paused for a moment and said
I loved and honored them
When they were humans
They would come to me
Swim and play, enjoy boating
Even worship their Gods
Standing knee deep in the water

I had freedom to flow as I liked
Run to the fields, farms and forests
Irrigate trees, plants — big and small
Nourishing them to grow timber
Fruits, flowers, vegetables, grains
Animals would freely come to me
Drink fresh water, take bath
Birds would sing on the branches of
Lush green trees on my banks
Sun, moon, stars and the sky
Would reflect their images onto me
Hot winds would become cool
After touching and kissing me
My majestic flow would inspire
Poets, philosophers, and singers

i am losing my appearance and glory
I have no love left for greedy humans
They are destroying my purity
Enslaving me by dams, reservoirs
Killing my colorful fishes, tortoises
Crocodiles and other species in my shelter
For their food and factories
Dumping waste, poisonous chemicals
Polluting me continuously, mercilessly

I had been warning them off and on
Flooding towns, cities farms and fields
Breaking dams and reservoirs
Creating scarcity of drinking water
But they have not learnt the lesson
If they fail to mend, I may think of
Destroying the civilizations built on
The four pillars of selfishness, greed
Cruelty and immorality
In the kingdom of God -
All objects of nature and all species
Have the same right to survive and
Live together as human beings.

The Light

When the fight is between
Darkness and light
The latter shines bright
Shows the way to
The boat of life
In turbulent waters
Gives hope and
Keeps depression at bay
Invites from the blue
A golden ray.

Cheers

Life a continuous phenomenon
Death a stop gap
What perishes is the body
Not the soul
An eternal indestructible light
Showing always the path bright
We reap what we sow
In this or successive life
Committing sins give pain
Doing good bring cheers.

Revolution, Revolution . . .

Where are Plato and Socrates?
Where are Lincoln and Gandhi?
We are told we are born free
We have rights the constitution gives
Parliament enacts, the judiciary guards

Kings and emperors are no more
We can elect government to
Protect and preserve our sovereignty
Promote welfare, create opportunities
Jobs, education and social security

TV, radio, internet, print media
Tell us wonderful things happening
Around us and in other parts of world
But have their hidden agenda too
Give us more views than the news

Provoked and misdirected by the media
We may act the way we should not
Those running the media may be bought
Paid to echo the their master's voice
Viewers, listeners left with little choice

Leaders' people elect and empower
Promise the moon but disappoint soon
Greed takes over needs, power corrupts
Servants become masters in no time
Indulging in coercion and crime

Companies capitalize at labor's cost
Bankers show investors a heaven
Invest, disinvest their funds recklessly
Ride on the tiger of the free market
Fail to check the fall eventually

Bureaucracy and red tape in government
Yes men surrounding the ministers
Judiciary delaying delivery of justice
Police harassing the innocent
People feeling insecure in the system

Living on the false promises of leaders
Shattered dreams and hopes belied
People look towards the agents of change
Writers, thinkers, poets, philosophers
To show the path, educate and inspire

Revolt against the corrupt regimes
Injustice, misrule wherever they are
In governance under the present system
May not be easy, but not impossible
When people awake, arise and fight.

Precious

All species are
Nature's precious creation
They need love
Care and protection.

Love Peace and Harmony

A saint was addressing
Men and women of different faiths
Colors, creeds and religions
An innocent man asked
When noble souls like you preach
Benevolence, charity and forgiveness
I wonder why the people do the opposite?
Why nations fight, terrorists blast?
Why millions are still poor and deprived?
Why neighbors' can't live in peace?
Why husband and wife divorce?

The saint smiled for a while and replied
My boy you know charity begins at home
Buddha forgave those who came to kill him
Jesus kissed the cross to save others
Gandhi walked the talk
When we peep into ourselves we find
Ego, ignorance, anger, envy, greed
Lust for power, status and money
Prompt us to behave in ways unpredictable
Create misunderstanding and conflict
Together we make a family, nation and world
If we can control ourselves and behave
Love, peace and harmony will prevail.